Creepy Crawlies

Pauline Cartwright

Contents

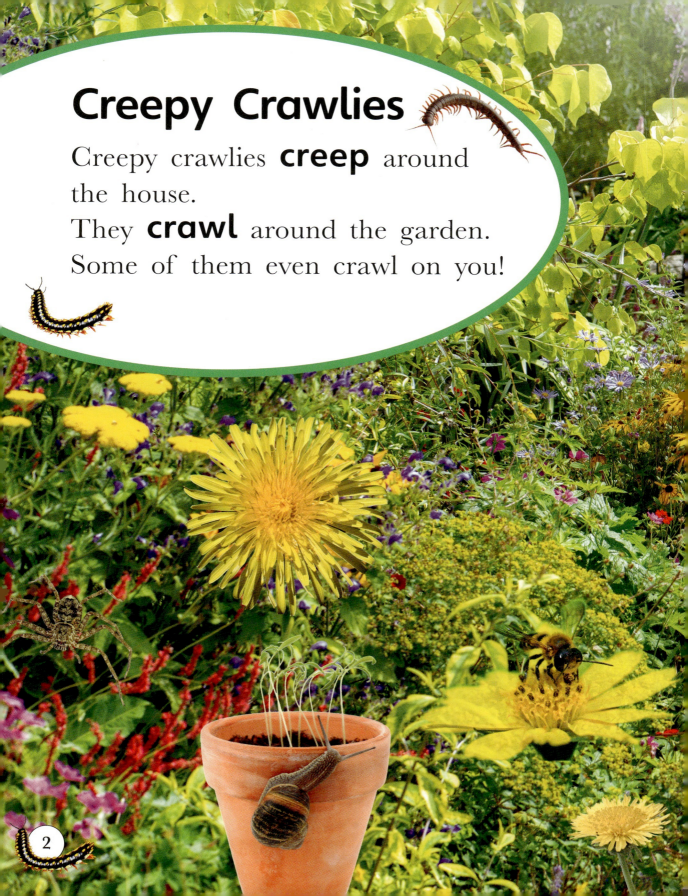

Creepy Crawlies

Creepy crawlies **creep** around the house.
They **crawl** around the garden.
Some of them even crawl on you!

In Your Garden

Look in a flowerbed.
You might see a beetle.

Beetles

Beetles have two lots of wings.
The top wings are hard, like a shell.

*The hard wings lift
up and the beetle
can fly!*

Lots of Legs

Look under a rock.
You might find a centipede or a millipede.

Millipedes and centipedes look alike, but they are different.

Centipede

Claws

Centipedes have claws on their head.

Millipede

Millipedes eat rotten leaves and plants.

Slimy!

Look at the garden path.
You might see a shiny trail.
It is a trail of **slime**!

Slugs and snails have no legs.
They glide along on slime.
The slime protects their bodies.
It helps them go up walls and trees.

Snail

Slug

In Your House

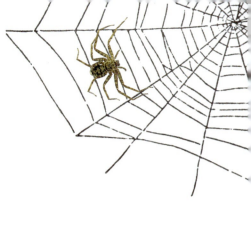

Look around you!

Spiders

Look up at the walls and roof.
You might see a spider!

Spiders spin webs from silk.
They wait for bugs to land
in their webs.

Creepy Fact

Spiders trap bugs with
silk, and then drink
their blood!

On You!

You may not see them, but there are lots of creepy crawlies on you and your pets!

Fleas

Fleas are very small insects that live on pets. Fleas bite pets and drink their blood.

13

Dust Mites

Dust mites are so small that you cannot even see them.

Dust mites eat dead skin. Yuck!

Creepy Fact

Dust mites like to live in your bed!

Creepy Fun!

Name the Creepy Crawlies

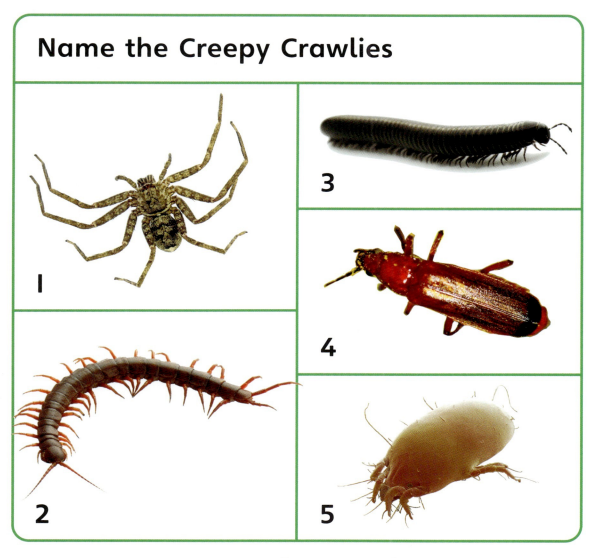

1

2

3

4

5

1. spider 2. centipede 3. millipede 4. beetle 5. dust mite

Index